BOOK 4

HEADWORK

Chris Culshaw and Deborah Waters

OXFORD UNIVERSITY PRESS

Oxford University Press, Walton Street, Oxford OX2 6DP

Oxford   London
New York   Toronto   Melbourne   Auckland
Kuala Lumpur   Singapore   Hong Kong   Tokyo
Delhi   Bombay   Calcutta   Madras   Karachi
Nairobi   Dar es Salaam   Cape Town

and associated companies in
Beirut   Berlin   Ibadan   Mexico City   Nicosia

Oxford is a trade mark of Oxford University Press

© Oxford University Press 1984

First published 1984

Reprinted 1984

ISBN 0 19 833375 7

Illustrations are by Andy Bylo,
Marie-Hélène Jeeves, Hugh Marshall,
David Murry, Ursula Sieger
and Shoo Rayner

The cover illustration is by
Marie-Hélène Jeeves

Typeset in Great Britain by
Rowland Phototypsetting Ltd
Bury St Edmunds, Suffolk
and printed by
R. J. Acford, Chichester

CONTENTS

Headwork is based on the following assumptions:

> that we learn to read by reading;
>
> that reading is in essence a problem solving process;
>
> that different types of reading matter demand different strategies.

The books have been written to help pupils find a challenge in the necessary routine of practising basic reading skills and to help them understand that reading involves thinking. We have therefore tried to balance readability against "thinkability" and posed demanding questions in an interesting but readable way.

Most of the tasks have a puzzle element and often ask the pupil to read with a specific question in mind. Some ask the learner to restructure what s/he has read by changing text into drawing. Some demand comparison between pictures or between texts. Some require summaries. Others involve sequencing. Many are designed to develop skills of classification and introduce different ways of tabulating information.

While many of the tasks lead to clear-cut, short (often single word) written answers, others are more open-ended and ask the pupil to use concepts such as "true", "false" and "not enough evidence" and later: "probably true", "probably false" and "definitely true" or "definitely false". These open-ended tasks lend themselves to oral work in pairs or in small groups.

There is constant repetition of basic sight words and concepts including colours, shapes, parts of the body, and terms that define position in time and space such as *over*, *under*, *next to*, *before*, *after*, *right*, *left*, etc.

In compiling *Headwork* we have been concerned above all to help learners in their efforts to *comprehend* what they read. So, text is supported with pictures and diagrams and new and difficult words are introduced in meaningful contexts.

"Readability" measures have many shortcomings and do not always do justice to the subtlety of the reading process. It is difficult to say exactly what makes a text readable and comprehensible: factors such as syntax, topic, concept loading, the match between the text and the readers' prior knowledge all play a part. Simple texts, with strictly controlled vocabulary, are not always the easiest to read with understanding. What is more, such texts offer very little challenge and may well defeat our ends for they are unlikely to get our pupils reading and *re-reading* in their efforts to search for meaning. There must be some challenge, some puzzlement and intellectual demand if the pupil is to develop into a reflective reader.

The table shows the major skills practised by each task. This is a broad categorization as the categories often overlap. For example, many of the matching tasks also require sequencing skills. The table also identifies those tasks which need a lot of teacher input, both in starting the learners off and in discussing their answers.

Major skills emphasized	page number
Cloze	44–45, 48–49, 55, 62
Drawing	ⓈⒺ, 46–47, ⑥④
Matching	8–9, 10, 24–25, 26, 28, 29, 30, 31 **32–33**, 40–41, **52–53**, 63
Deduction	6–7, 11, 14–15, 16–17, 27, ㉟, 37, 38–39, 46–47, 53, ㊽–㊼, 58–59, 60–61
Sequencing	18–19, 50, 54
Classification	34, 36, 51
Flow charts	12–13, 20–21, 62
Solving riddles	42–43
Comparison	22–23
Writing	29, 30

Numbers printed in **bold** indicate tasks needing a lot of teacher explanation.
Numbers circled indicate tasks with open-ended outcomes and a number of possible answers.

What to do

Are the sentences true or false?

1. The warthog's top speed is 30 mph.
2. The zebra can catch the gazelle.
3. The lion can catch the springbok.
4. The spotted hyena can catch the gazelle.
5. The giraffe and the buffalo have the same top speed.
6. The ostrich can run as fast as the lion.

7. The springbok is the second fastest animal.
8. The gazelle can run twice as fast as the white rhinoceros.
9. Only one other animal can travel as fast as the springbok.
10. The ostrich can travel 10 mph faster than the springbok.
11. The giraffe's top speed is 10 mph less than the buffalo's top speed.
12. All the animals with a top speed of 50 mph have four legs.
13. Only one animal can catch the cheetah.
14. The gnu can travel twice as far as the elephant in one hour.

DEDUCTION

Giraffe 30 mph

Elephant 25 mph

White rhinoceros 25 mph

Hunting dog 30 mph

Buffalo 35 mph

Spotted hyena 40 mph

Zebra 40 mph

Warthog 30 mph

Gazelle 50 mph

Lion 50 mph

Gnu 50 mph

Ostrich 50 mph

Springbok 60 mph

Cheetah 70 mph

DEDUCTION

Ten rules for swimmers

1. Stay out of the water if sharks have been seen in your area.
2. Do not swim in muddy water.
3. Do not swim on your own.
4. Do not swim at night.
5. If you see a shark, do not panic.
   Try to swim quietly, with even strokes.
6. If you see a shark, keep in a horizontal position.   Do not let your legs dangle.
7. If you see a shark, do not turn your back on it.   Try to keep it in view.
8. Sharks are attracted by blood.
   Do not swim with an open cut.
9. It is best to wear a swim suit to match your skin colour.   Sharks can see colours.
10. You are more likely to be attacked in WARM water.

What to do

Here are reports of eight shark attacks.   The eight swimmers were attacked because they did not follow the safety rules for swimmers.
Which rules did each swimmer break?   (Some may have broken more than one rule.)

Write your answers like this: A. *Gordon broke rule number* . . . . .

Report A

Gordon was swimming with three friends very late at night.   He was attacked by a shark not far from the lighthouse.

Report B

Tony was on holiday in America. He cut his foot on the beach. He went swimming the same day and got attacked.

Report C

Doug was attacked by a large shark. He was swimming by himself. He was diving for starfish.

Report D

Santi saw a notice on the beach. It said that sharks had been seen nearby. She wasn't scared of sharks so she went with her brothers for a swim. She was attacked and killed.

Report E

John was in the water with two girls. He saw a big shark nearby. He shouted and waved his arms. The shark attacked him but not the girls.

Report F

Bernadette always went swimming on the far side of the beach. The sea was very warm there. She was attacked when she was with her sisters.

Report G

Carlton was very keen to do some diving. The water was not clear. Carlton went in on his own. He wanted to test his new air tanks.

Report H

Sheila was a very good swimmer. She bought a new, bright red wet suit. She was swimming with some friends when a shark attacked her.

What to do

Look at the picture.   Say who lives in each house.

Write your answers like this:

Frances Webb, Malcolm Webb and Mrs. Webb – No 6

A.   My name is Frances Webb.   I live with my mum and brother, Malcolm.   We live in a semi-detached house.   Last year my mum built a garage.

B.   My granny lives next door to us.   She lives in a bungalow.

C.   My best friend is George Kelly.   He lives next door but one to us.   He lives in a terraced house.

D.   Next door to George lives Mrs Jenkinson.   She has a lodger called Mr Hutchinson.

E.   The Patel family live in a detached house.   It has a big garage at the front.   Mr and Mrs Patel have three children, Ravi, Kamala and Prem.

F.   My Uncle Tom lives next door to the Patels.   He lives with my two cousins, Becky and Jane.

G.   That leaves Mr and Miss Hart.   They live next door to us.   Miss Hart is kind but her brother is mean.

MATCHING

Mrs. Golding is 68.   She lives alone with 14 cats.   She lives in a tiny village in Yorkshire.   She was born there and she has lived there all her life.

Before she was married, she was a nurse.   After she was married, she became the village post-mistress.   She does not work now, but sometimes she helps out behind the bar at the *Red Lion* pub.   She was married to a window cleaner called Tom.   He died when he fell off a ladder last year.

She has a son called John.   He lives in Canada where he works as a doctor.

Mrs. Golding has two hobbies: horse riding and fishing.

What to do

Read the description of Mrs. Golding.
Say if these statements are:

Definitely true *(D.T.)*   Probably true *(P.T.)*
Definitely false *(D.F.)*   Probably false *(P.F.)*

1. She cannot read or write.
2. She is nervous about meeting people.
3. She has two grand-children.
4. She likes animals.
5. She knows a lot about first aid.
6. She is always ill.
7. She lives in a very big house.
8. She does not believe in God.
9. She has been a widow for 10 years.
10. Her house is near a cinema.

DEDUCTION

A

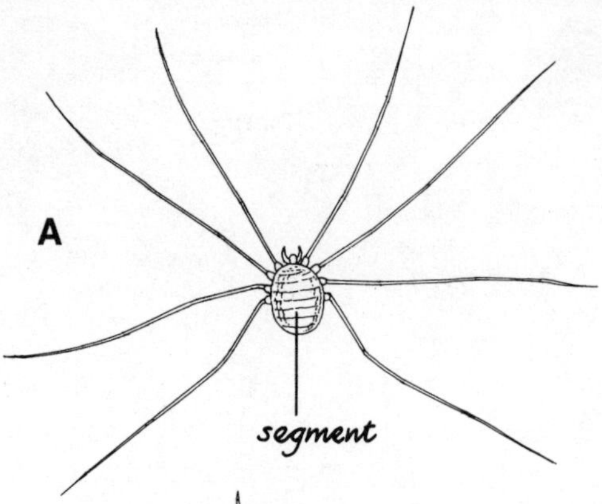
segment

B

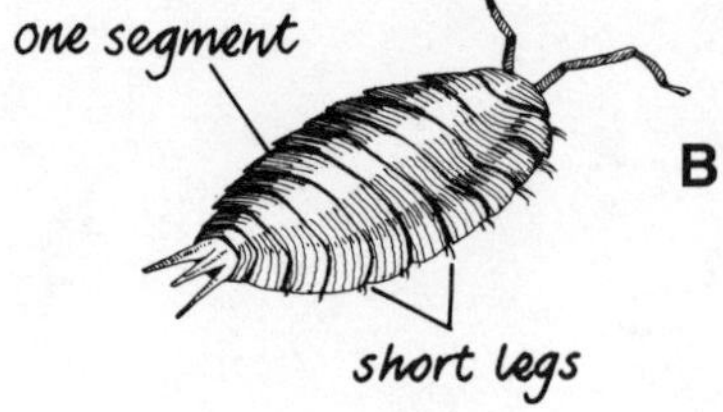
one segment
short legs

C

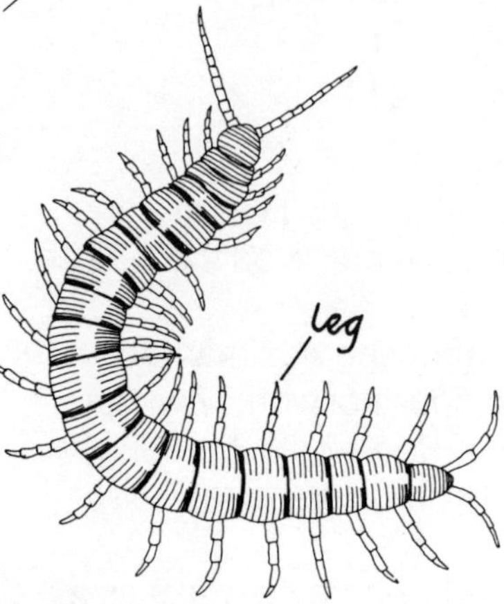
leg

D

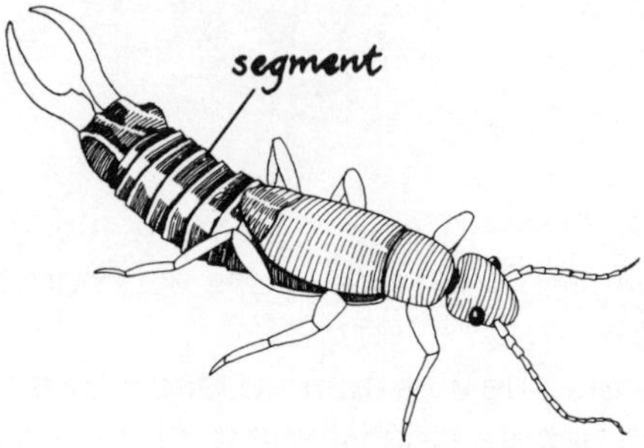
segment

E

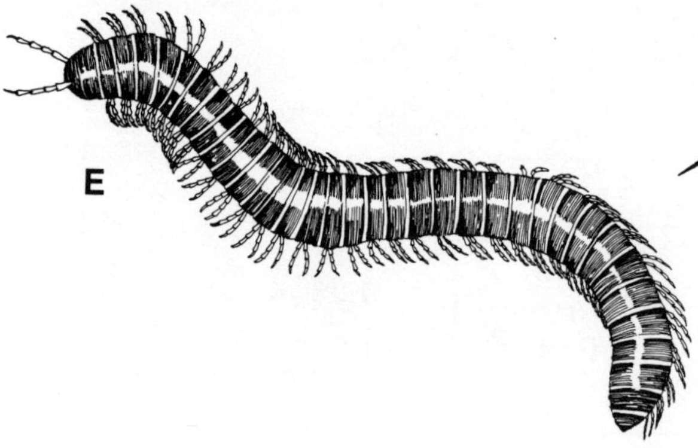

F

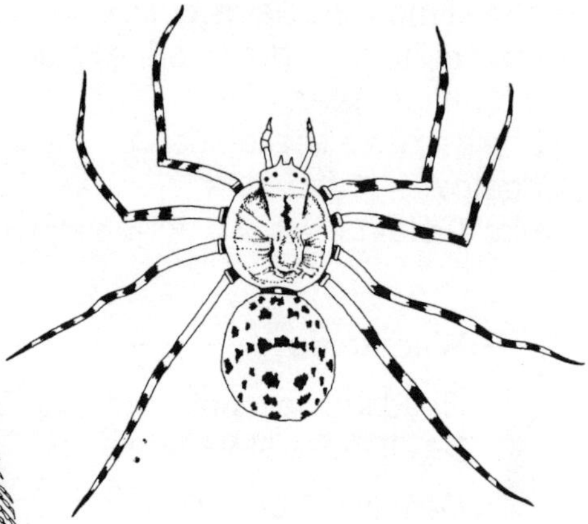

What to do

Look at animal A. Follow the arrows on the key to find out its name.
Now look at animal B and do the same.
Do the same for all the animals.

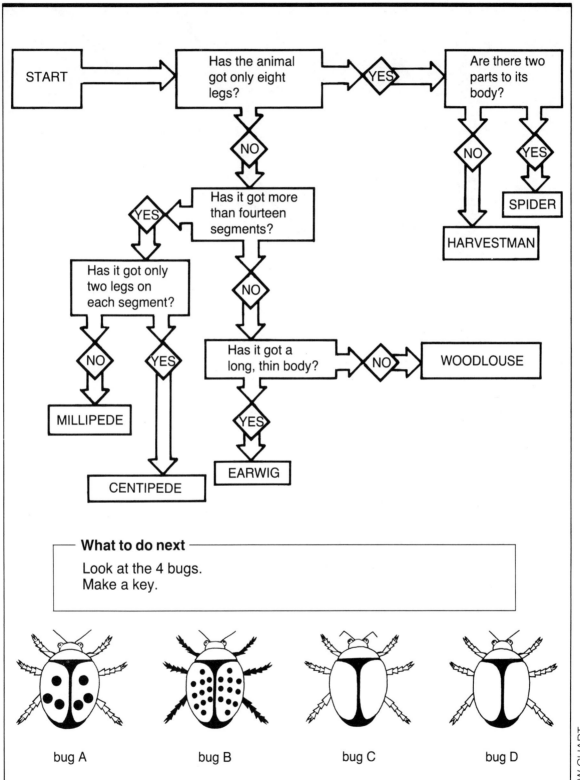

START

Has the animal got only eight legs?

YES → Are there two parts to its body?

NO ↓

Has it got more than fourteen segments?

YES ←

NO → Has it got two parts to its body?
- NO → HARVESTMAN
- YES → SPIDER

Has it got only two legs on each segment?
- NO → MILLIPEDE
- YES → CENTIPEDE

Has it got a long, thin body?
- NO → WOODLOUSE
- YES → EARWIG

What to do next

Look at the 4 bugs.
Make a key.

bug A   bug B   bug C   bug D

CLIFFTOWN

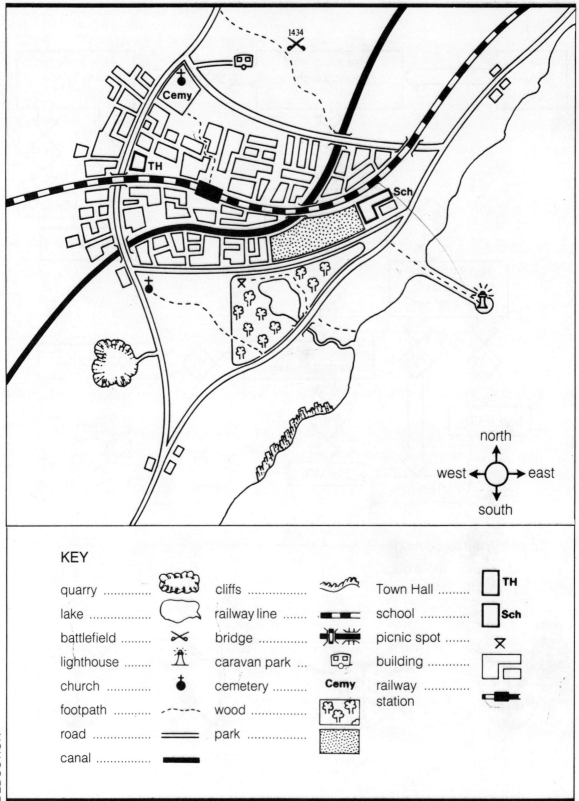

KEY

quarry	cliffs	Town Hall .... **TH**
lake	railway line	school .... **Sch**
battlefield	bridge	picnic spot ....
lighthouse	caravan park ...	building ....
church	cemetery .... **Cemy**	railway .... station
footpath	wood	
road	park	
canal		

north
west ← → east
south

1. There is a picnic spot in the wood.
2. There is a lake in the park.
3. One of the churches is near a caravan park.
4. There is a footpath from the school to the lighthouse.
5. The town hall was built in 1435.

6. There are four bridges over water on the map.
7. The cliffs are very dangerous.
8. There are graveyards next to both churches.
9. There is a swimming pool at the school.
10. Both the churches are near road junctions.

11. The railway line crosses the canal next to the town hall.
12. The canal goes under the railway line next to the park.
13. One of the footpaths goes from the railway to the battlefield.
14. The footpath from the railway station leads to the cemetery.
15. To get from the town hall to the quarry you must cross the canal.

16. The school is west of the wood.
17. The railway station is south of the caravan park.
18. The railway crosses the canal north of the park.
19. The stream from the lake runs into the sea just south of the cliffs.
20. If you walk east from the church near the quarry, you will come to the lake in the wood.

DEDUCTION

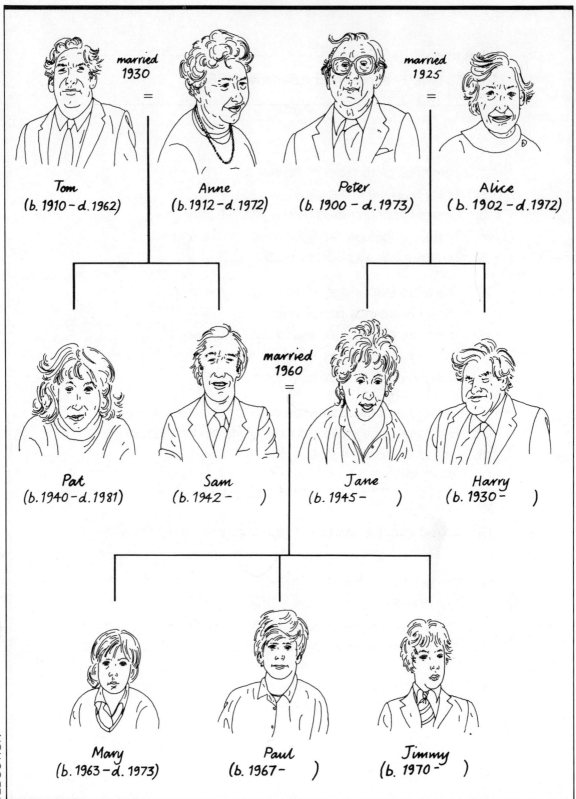

Tom
(b. 1910 – d. 1962)

married 1930
=

Anne
(b. 1912 – d. 1972)

Peter
(b. 1900 – d. 1973)

married 1925
=

Alice
(b. 1902 – d. 1972)

Pat
(b. 1940 – d. 1981)

Sam
(b. 1942 –   )

married 1960
=

Jane
(b. 1945 –   )

Harry
(b. 1930 –   )

Mary
(b. 1963 – d. 1973)

Paul
(b. 1967 –   )

Jimmy
(b. 1970 –   )

DEDUCTION

Look at the family tree.
Are these statements true or false?

1.   Sam married Jane.
2.   Paul is Sam's son.
3.   Peter married Anne.
4.   Pat is Peter's daughter.
5.   Harry is Alice's only son.

6.   Paul and Jimmy are twin brothers.
7.   Tom and Alice are brother and sister.
8.   Jane is Paul's mother.
9.   Harry is Jimmy's uncle.
10.   Pat is Mary's grandmother.

11.   Alice is Paul's grandmother.
12.   Jimmy is Tom's grandson.
13.   Paul is Harry's nephew.
14.   Mary is Peter's niece.
15.   Pat and Jane are sisters-in-law.

16.   Tom and Jane were married in 1930.
17.   Mary was born in 1973.
18.   Peter was born in 1900.
19.   Mary was only ten years old when she died.
20.   Paul was four years old when his brother was born.

Danny saw a sheep trapped on a ledge. He had to rescue it, or it might have fallen off the ledge and drowned in the sea.

He used these six things to rescue the sheep.

What to do

How did Danny rescue the sheep?
Look at the drawings.
Put the sentences in the right order.

Write your answers like this: *1.C*

A.   He tied the walking stick to one end of the rope.
B.   When the sheep was eating the apple, Danny lowered the walking stick very slowly down the cliff.
C.   Danny put the rope over a branch of the tree.
D.   He hooked the walking stick under the sheep's horns.
E.   Danny tied the apple to the cotton.
F.   The log fell down the cliff and the sheep was pulled up.
G.   Danny tied the heavy log to the other end of the rope.
H.   He lowered the apple down to the sheep.
I.   He pushed the heavy log off the cliff.

What to do

Use the flow chart to name each insect.

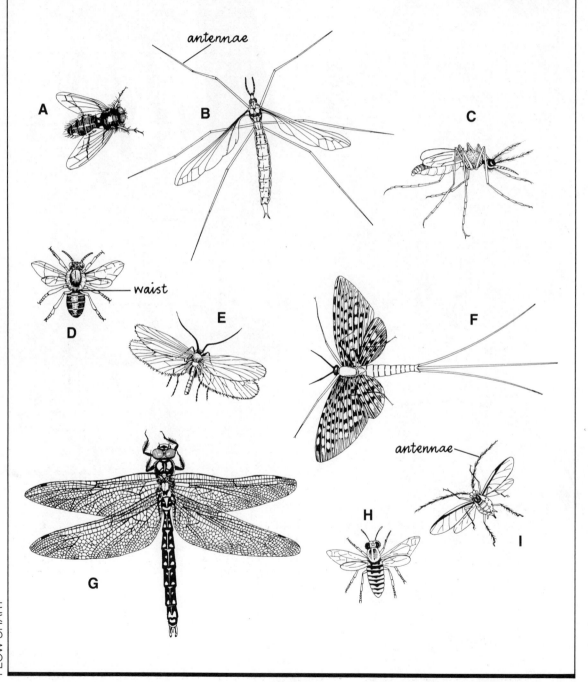

antennae

A

B

C

waist

D

E

F

antennae

G

H

I

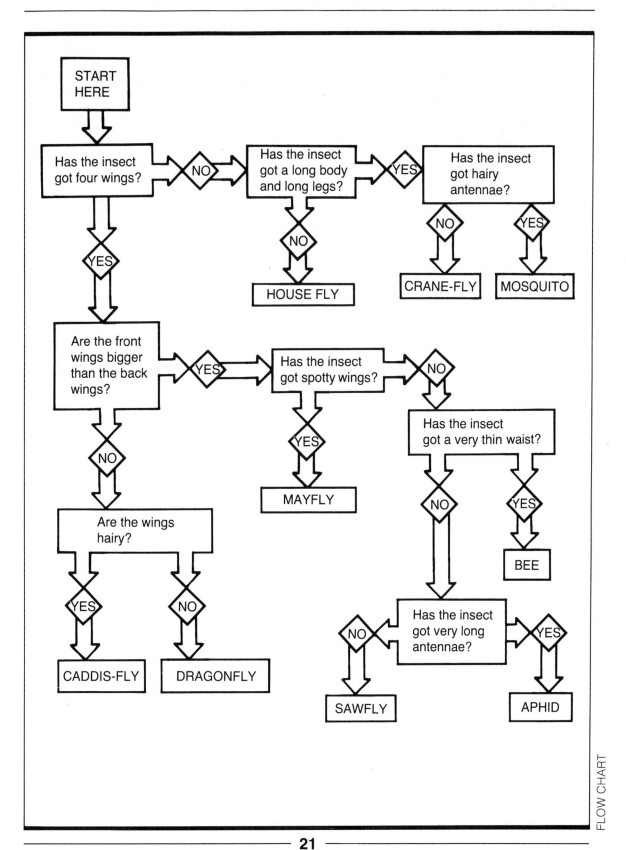

What to do

After the accident, the policeman asked six witnesses what they had seen.   Only one witness made a correct statement.   The other five witnesses all made one mistake.
Which is the correct statement?   Can you spot the one mistake in each of the other statements?   What are they?

Witness A

"I was standing on the corner at about ten o'clock.   I heard a crash.   The Blackpool bus ran into the milk van.   The milkman fell out on to the street.   He was unconscious. And there was milk all over the road."

Witness B

"I was on my way to the butcher's when it happened.   I heard the sound of breaking glass.   I thought it was a smash and grab raid.   I ran round the corner.   The bus had run straight into the front of the van.   What a mess!"

COMPARISON

Witness C

"I didn't see it properly, because I need new glasses. The Preston bus had just pulled away from the stop. The milk van shot out in front of it. What an idiot! He's lucky to be alive. It happened about eleven o'clock, I think."

Witness D

"I was just across the road when it happened. The milk van was coming out of the side street. He didn't see the bus. The bus driver tried to stop. The milkman jumped out just in time."

Witness E

"This is a very dangerous corner. This is the second accident we've had here in a week. The Preston bus was going too fast. And it was a woman bus driver. They are a menace to the public!'

Witness F

"The milkman was hurt. It was me who called the ambulance. The bus hit the side of the milk van. I don't know what caused the accident. It happened about a quarter to ten. I was on my way to the dentist. I've missed my appointment now because of this accident."

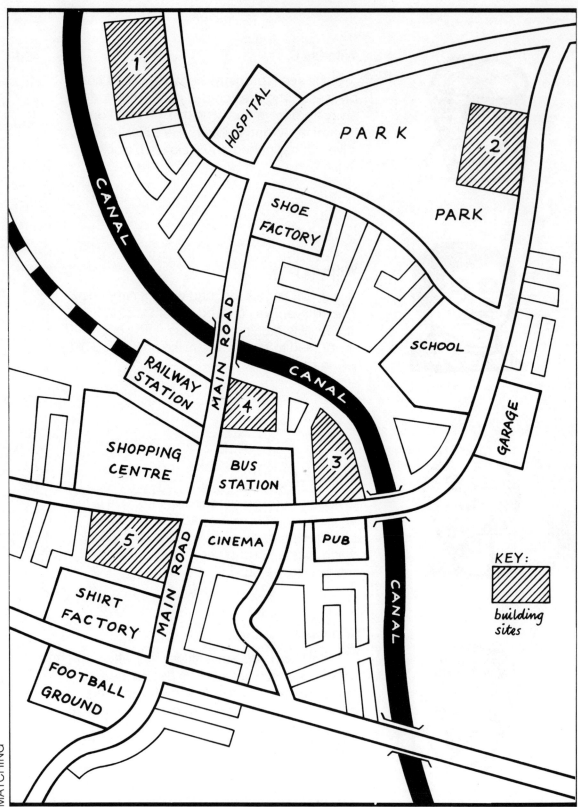

I want to build an old people's home. I need a site in a quiet street that no heavy lorries come down.

Builder A.

I want to build a canoe club where kids can make canoes and learn to use them. The site has to be quite near the bus and railway stations because most kids don't have cars.

I want to build a day nursery for toddlers. There has to be a nice safe place for them to play nearby. The site has got to be near the shoe factory because lots of the toddlers' mums work there.

Builder B.

Builder C.

I want to build a fish and chip shop. I'm looking for a site near the busy part of town. It must be quite near the school as well, because lots of pupils like chips for lunch.

I want to build a car park. Lots of people come to our town to do their shopping. Lots of fans come to watch United play too.

Builder D.

Builder E.

What to do next

If you were a builder, where would you build a library and an indoor swimming pool?   Give a reason for the places you chose.

MATCHING

ZODIAC

Aquarius January 21–Feb 20	Gemini May 21–June 20	Libra September 21–Oct 20	Taurus April 21–May 20
The weather will play an important part in your plans.	You will find some cash – then lose it.	Watch out for the postman – and a nasty shock.	Your plans will be upset by family problems.
Pisces February 21–March 20	**Cancer** June 21–July 20	**Scorpio** October 21–Nov 20	**Virgo** August 21–Sept 20
Nothing will go right for you today.	You will go on an important trip today.	A four-footed friend may surprise you today.	Red is your lucky colour today.
Aries March 21–April 20	**Leo** July 21–August 20	**Sagittarius** November 21–Dec 20	**Capricorn** December 21–Jan 20
You will have a good day at school today.	A friend may let you down today.	You may be in a fix, but a stranger will help you out.	Look out – you may lose a friend.

What to do

Look at the horoscope.
Suppose that everyone's horoscope came true. Can you work out each person's birth sign?
Write your answer like this: *1. Kamala's birth sign is Taurus.*

1. Kamala wanted to go to the school disco, but her mum would not let her go.
2. Julie went to London to see about a new job.
3. Paul was picked for the rugby team, but the match was washed out by a thunder storm.
4. Tina got a red racing bike for her birthday.
5. Pete's car broke down, but a woman stopped and helped him to fix it.
6. David found 50p. but then he dropped it and it rolled down a grid.
7. Sally lost her cat.
8. John got 10/10 for his apple pie in cookery.
9. Harry fell off a ladder and hurt his leg. The ladder fell on the greenhouse and smashed ten windows.
10. Winston could not play chess. His partner did not turn up.
11. Joan found out that her dog was going to have pups.
12. Jane got a gas bill for £63.37 in the post.

MATCHING

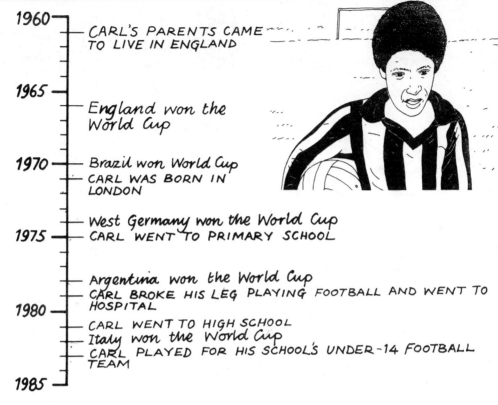

1960 — CARL'S PARENTS CAME TO LIVE IN ENGLAND

1965 —

England won the World Cup

1970 — Brazil won World Cup
— CARL WAS BORN IN LONDON

— West Germany won the World Cup
1975 — CARL WENT TO PRIMARY SCHOOL

— Argentina won the World Cup
— CARL BROKE HIS LEG PLAYING FOOTBALL AND WENT TO HOSPITAL
1980 —
— CARL WENT TO HIGH SCHOOL
— Italy won the World Cup
— CARL PLAYED FOR HIS SCHOOL'S UNDER-14 FOOTBALL TEAM

1985 —

What to do

Look at the time line. Are the sentences true(T), false(F) or is there not enough evidence(NEE)?

1. Carl was born in 1970.
2. Carl was born in Jamaica.
3. Carl's mum and dad went to see the 1966 World Cup final at Wembley.
4. Carl broke his leg when he was at the High School.
5. Carl was 12 years old when he was picked for the High School Under-14 football team.
6. Carl went to Spain to see the 1982 World Cup.
7. When Carl was in hospital with a broken leg he watched the final of the 1978 World Cup on TV.
8. Carl was 3 three years old when West Germany won the World Cup.
9. Brazil won the World Cup one year after Carl was born.
10. Italy won the World Cup two years before Carl went to High School.

DEDUCTION

snake · turtle · bird · sun · moon · snow · wolf

fish · canoe · horse or pony · cloud · sky · river or lake · reeds or grass

rain · axe · flower · reindeer · woman · man · buffalo

What to do

Use the key to match the picture with its meaning.

Write your answer like this: *1 E*

1. Red Hand was killed by a buffalo.
2. Red Hand lay in the snow for a day and a night.
3. Red Hand saw a wolf by the river.
4. White Star took two days to cross the great lake.
5. That night, Red Hand met White Star by the river.
6. White Star killed a wolf by the river.

Red Hand

White Star

A

B

C

D

E

F

MATCHING

What to do next

Read the story.
The four pictures below tell the same story.   One picture is missing.   Work out the missing picture.
Draw it in your own book.

There was a very bad snow storm.   It went on for three days.   After the storm, Red Hand went to look for some food.   He rode for two days, but found nothing to eat.   That night, Red Hand was asleep by a river.   A wolf attacked him.   Red Hand killed the wolf and took the meat back to his tribe.

Red Hand

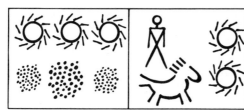

What to do next

Here is a story in pictures.   Write the story in words.   This is how the story starts.   Finish it in your own words.

How Red Hand died

One day, Red Hand was on his pony, hunting.   His pony stood on a snake.   The snake killed the pony.   Red Hand fell to the ground.   He lay there for two days ....

White Star

Red Hand

MATCHING/WRITING

What to do

This is a story told in pictures.   You have to write the story in words.   This is how to start it.   You have to finish it in your own words.

The flower

Red Hand and White Star were brother and sister.   One day, Red Hand was bitten by a snake.   He was dying.   White Star had to find a special flower to make him well again.   She set off on her pony to look for this flower.   She rode for two days.   That night, when she was asleep ....

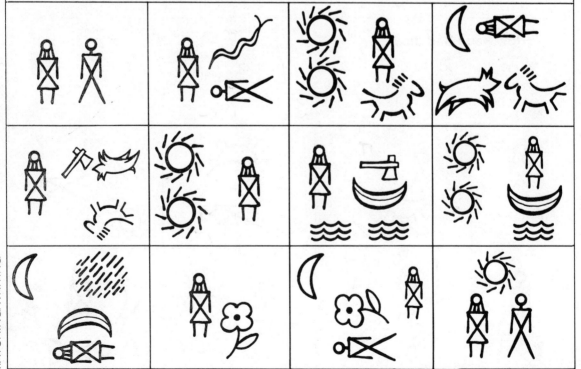

What to do

Match the pictures with the bits of the story.
Write your answers like this: 1. C

1. It was the worst drought there had ever been. It had not rained for weeks. No plants could grow. The animals were dying of thirst. The people were hungry.

2. Silver Fox saw that the people were dying. She had to help them get food.

3. Silver Fox walked for two days. She saw a buffalo. She tried to kill it with her axe but it ran off.

4. Two days later, she met a man called Tall Tree. He told Silver Fox where she could find some fish. He said she could use his canoe.

5. Silver Fox walked on until she came to a lake. She saw Tall Tree's canoe. She caught two big, silver fish.

6. That night, as Silver Fox was sleeping, a wolf came. It wanted the fish.

7. Silver Fox killed it with her axe.

8. Then Silver Fox walked back to her village. She walked for a day and a night.

9. The people were very ill, but when they had the fish they got better.

10. That night it rained very hard. The plants started to grow again. There was food for the people and water for all the animals.

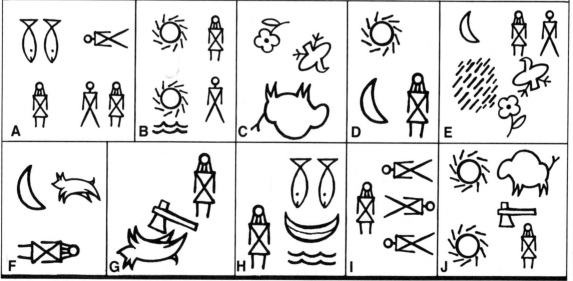

MATCHING

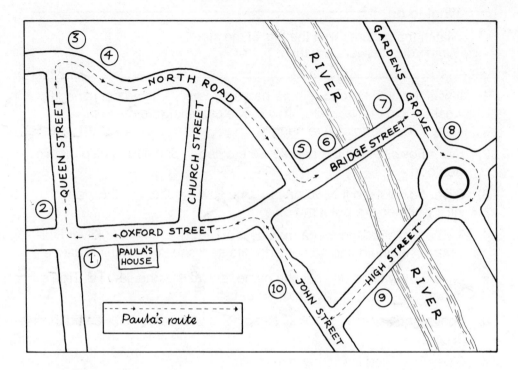

What to do

Paula went for a ride on her bike.   The map shows her route. Underneath there is a description of her route.   Which road signs did she see and where?   Write your answers like this:

1. ⚠

Paula turned left when she came out of her house.   She rode to the end of the road and turned right at the cross roads.   Queen Street was very bumpy so she had to slow down.   When she got to the end, she turned right into North Road.   She had to stop quickly, because someone was crossing on the zebra crossing.

She had to change gear to get up the steep hill.   When she got to Bridge Street, she wanted to turn right but she couldn't.   She turned left instead.   She thought she might have to wait at the river.   She was lucky and she rode straight over the bridge.   The road was very wet and slippery.   Paula then turned right along Gardens Grove.   She took the third turning off the roundabout.   She went over the river and passed a school.   She turned right into John Street.   The road got very narrow. At the end of the road she turned left.   She was back home.

MATCHING

cross roads

children going to
or from school

pedestrian
crossing

uneven road

no left turn

road narrows
on both sides

slippery road

no right turn

steep hill
downwards

roundabout

swing bridge

steep hill
upwards

Polly and May are sisters. They went on holiday together. They stayed with their Aunty Kath. These bar charts show what they did on their holiday.

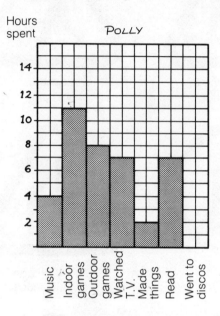

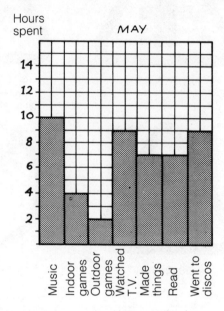

Polly and May's aunty is very rich. At the end of the holiday, she bought the girls some presents. These are the presents she bought.

1. Track suit
2. Record
3. Tool kit
4. Chess set
5. Bright red T-shirt
6. Guitar
7. Fishing rod

8. Roller boots
9. Pair of trainers
10. High heeled shoes
11. Cookery book
12. Very tight jeans
13. Video game
14. Book of horror stories

What to do

Use the bar charts to work out which girl got which presents.

Write your answers like this: *1. Polly*

CLASSIFICATION

Barbara was digging in her garden. She dug up some old bones. She cleaned them and laid them out in the yard. This is what they looked like.

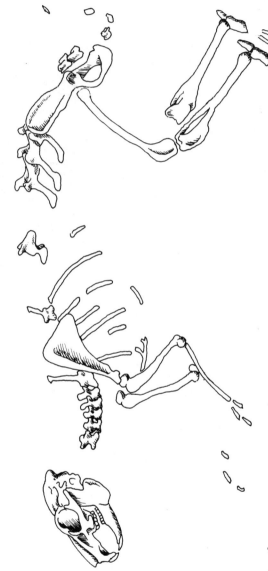

What to do

Trace the bones.
Complete the skeleton by adding a few more bones.
What do you think the animal looked like?
Use the skeleton to help you make a drawing of the animal.
Write a description of your animal.
Use these words:

fur	claws	teeth	fore legs
ears	skull	tail	hind legs
markings		diet	habitat

DEDUCTION/DRAWING

What to do

We asked fifteen pupils what kind of things they worried about.
This is what they said.
Copy the table.   Classify the answers.

1. I always worry about tests.   I hate them.
2. I don't have any friends.   I worry about that.
3. I worry about Mum and Dad splitting up.
4. I worry about war, and atom bombs.
5. I worry about my pet dog.
6. I never worry.   I'm always happy.
7. I worry about hospitals and the dentist.
8. I worry about everything.   I'm a nervous person.
9. I worry about getting into fights.   I'm a coward.
10. I know it's daft but I'm scared of the dark.
11. I can't swim.   I worry about drowning.
12. I worry about school work.   I'm no good at maths.
13. I worry when I go in a lift.   I hate being shut in.
14. My dad lost his job in June.   I worry about money.
15. I worry about all the people starving in the world.

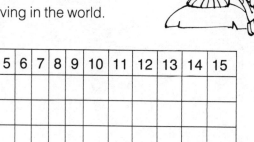

	1	2	3	4	5	6	7	8	9	10	11	12	13	14	15
Personal problems															
Family problems															
School problems	✓														
World problems															

Harry Coles was the fattest kid in the school. He didn't have any mates. He played by himself most times. He lived in the middle of town in a tall block of flats. About a mile from Harry's flat were hundreds of old houses. They were all empty. They were going to be pulled down so that new houses could be built. Harry liked playing about in the old houses. His dad told him to keep away from them. He said they were dangerous.

One Friday, on his way home from school, Harry went into one of the old, empty houses. He saw a door leading down into a small dark cellar. Harry went into the cellar to see what he could find. Just then he heard a terrific crash. The roof of the old house had fallen in. Harry tried to open the cellar door. It was stuck. Harry was trapped in the cellar ......

What to do

Here are five endings for the story. Only one fits the story.
Find the right ending.
Say why the other four do not fit.

Ending A

Harry looked round the cellar. He saw a small gap in the wall. He crawled out and ran home. He did not tell anyone about his lucky escape.

Ending B

There were lots of old newspapers in the cellar. Harry set the papers on fire. An hour later he was rescued by a policeman who saw the smoke.

Ending C

Peter Roberts, Harry's best mate, came looking for Harry. He heard Harry's shouts for help and pulled him out.

Ending D

Harry was rescued three days later by some policemen who used tracker dogs to find him.

Ending E

Harry shouted very loud, "Help! Help!" Luckily Harry's dad was in their back yard hanging out the washing. He heard Harry's cry for help and rescued him from the old house.

DEDUCTION

What to do

Look at the bar charts and say if the statements are true(T), false(F), or if there is not enough evidence(NEE).

About bar chart A

1. A mouse can live for three years.
2. Alligators don't live for as long as ostriches.
3. Women usually live longer than men.
4. Both the reptiles live longer than the bird.
5. Rhinos live longer than both men and women.
6. Some small animals don't live for very long.
7. Dolphins live longer than people.
8. Trout live only a short time *because* they live in water.

About bar chart B

9. The fastest animal is the cheetah.
10. Tortoises are the slowest animals.
11. Trout can swim at 20 mph.
12. An ostrich can overtake a jack rabbit.
13. The animal with the longest legs can run the fastest.
14. All the water animals on the chart are slower than the land animals.
15. All the birds in the world live for longer than all the fish.

About both bar charts

16. The slowest animal can live for one hundred years.
17. The animal that can run at 50 mph can live for fifty years.
18. The jack rabbit does not live very long *because* it runs fast.

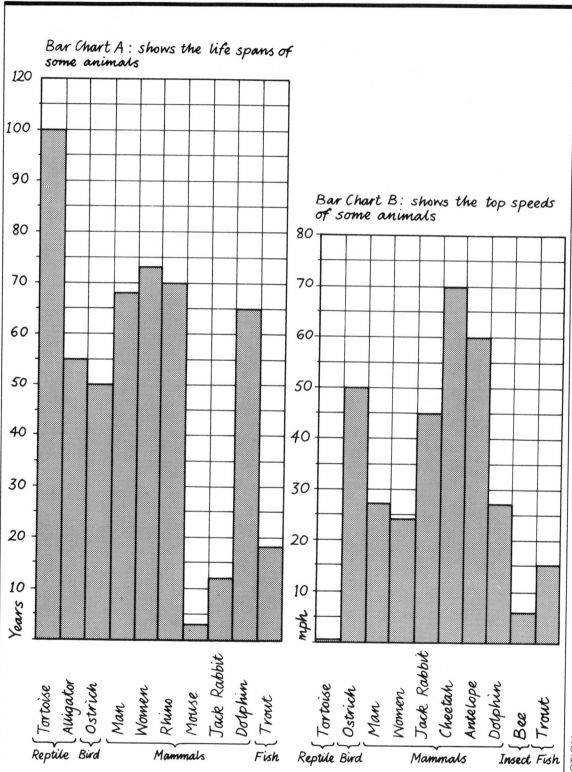

Bar Chart A: shows the life spans of some animals

Bar Chart B: shows the top speeds of some animals

1. Three small children are saved from a burning house.
2. Police are looking for the owners of stolen goods.
3. A small fire breaks out at a local school.
4. A fire starts in a car on the motorway.
5. A local man was run over by a bus.

6. A local woman died on the Isle of Man.
7. A girl was knocked off her bike by a car.
8. Girls and boys from a local school go on a sponsored bike ride.
9. A magpie attacked babies in their prams.
10. An old lady had her bag stolen on the bus.

11. A 14 year old youth stole some tools.
12. A search starts for a man who attacked a shopkeeper.
13. A woman dug up a human skull in her garden.
14. A house painter was taken to court for attacking a woman.
15. The barman at a local pub did a parachute jump to get money for charity.

┌─ **What to do next**

Now invent six new headlines.

Choose one and write its story.

A. Blaze damage to moving car

B. Skullduggery!

C. Blaze in bin

D. Any of this loot yours?

E. Man hurt in road mishap

F. Cyclist hurt in collision

G. Bully bird zaps babies

H. Pedal power pays

I. HANDBAG SNATCH

J. Man tipped can of paint over woman

K. POLICE HUNT KNIFE RAIDER

L. Three are saved from choking smoke

M. 'Bored' boy broke into workshop

N. £300 in pub para-leap

O. Island holiday ends in death

What to do

Read the conversations.
What are Bev and Lee talking about?
Write down the eight things.

1. **Near a church**
   Bev   Is this the one?
   Lee   Yes.
   Bev   How do you know?   I can't read the name.
   Lee   Look, you can just make out the letters S . . . M . . .
   Bev   Oh yes.   It says 'SMITH'.
   Lee   Yes.   That was my grandad's name.

2. **Outside a pet shop**
   Bev   Which one shall we buy?
   Lee   I like the black one.
   Bev   Will it be strong enough?
   Lee   Yes, I think so.
   Bev   It looks a bit weak to me.
   Lee   What about that brown one?
   Bev   Yes, that looks stronger.
   Lee   We need a very strong one.
   Bev   Why?
   Lee   If it breaks, Tim will run off and we might never find him
          again.

3. **At school (outside)**
   Lee   Who broke it?
   Bev   I don't know . . . vandals I suppose.
   Lee   What a drag!
   Bev   We can't play our match now.
   Lee   What a mess!
   Bev   There must have been a gang of them.   The wood is very thick.
   Lee   They could have used a saw.
   Bev   No, you can see where the wood has been snapped.

4. **In Lee's bedroom**
   Bev   What's wrong with it?   It sounds terrible.
   Lee   Ugh . . . there is jam all over it.
   Bev   No wonder it won't play.   Who did it?
   Lee   I bet it was my little brother.   Just wait until I get hold of him.

5. In the garden
   Lee   Can I have a go?
   Bev   Okay, but don't let my mum see it.
   Lee   Why not?
   Bev   I pinched the elastic from her sewing box.
   Lee   I'll see if I can hit that tree. (CRASH)
   Bev   Oh . . . no . . . you've hit the greenhouse.

6. On the bus
   Lee   Hey, look what I have found.
   Bev   Where were they?
   Lee   Down behind the seat.
   Bev   I wonder who they belong to?   Is there a name in the case?
   Lee   No.   What shall I do with them?
   Bev   Hand them to the driver when we get off.

7. In the bathroom
   Lee   Where is it?
   Bev   I don't know.   I saw the cat playing with it yesterday.
   Lee   Is it under the bath mat?
   Bev   No.   Perhaps it has rolled downstairs.
   Lee   Can you look for it please?   I can't have my bath until I find it.

8. In the kitchen
   Bev   It's no good.   I can't get it to work.
   Lee   Let me try.   I've got a strong grip.
   Bev   We shall be in trouble if it doesn't work.
   Lee   Why?
   Bev   I told Mum I would have tea ready when she came home from
         work.
   Lee   You're right.   It does not work.   It just goes round and round
         and nothing happens.
   Bev   Is there another one anywhere?
   Lee   Yes.   I've got one on my pen-knife.

What to do

Find the missing words.

Write your answers like this: *1. valve*

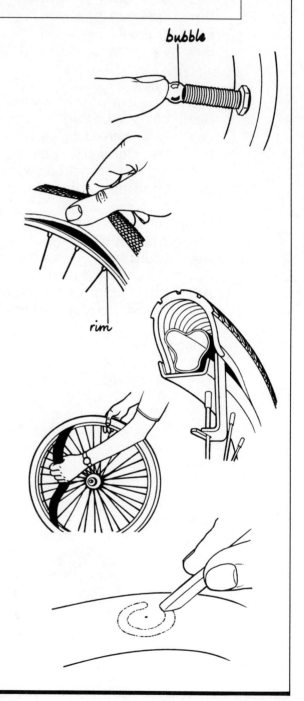

bubble

rim

First check the valve. Wet your finger and put it on the
    1   . If you see a
    2   , the valve is leaking. You may need to buy a new tube.

Take the   **3**   off the bike. Let the tyre down. Do this by taking the valve out or pushing down the centre pin.

Pinch the tyre away from the
    4   . Do this all the way round the wheel.

Put a tyre lever between the rim and the tyre. Put another
    5   a bit further round. Lever the tyre off the rim. Use levers to free a third of the tyre. The rest can be done by hand.

Take the inner tube out.

Look for the   **6**   . If you cannot see one, put the tube in some   **7** . Bubbles will come out from the hole. Put your finger over the hole. Mark it with some chalk.

Roughen the place around the hole with ___8___ .

Spread rubber cement around the hole.   Wait until the cement is tacky.   Cut a ___9___ of the right size.   Take the backing paper off the patch.   Put the patch over the hole and ___10___ hard.

Cover the patch with ___11___ to dry the uncovered cement.

___12___ that there is nothing sharp inside the tyre.

Pump a little air into the ___13___ .   Push the tube into the tyre.   Pull the valve through the hole in the wheel rim.

Push the tyre ___14___ the wheel rim.   Start at the valve. Do this on both sides.   The second side will be much more difficult.   Try not to use levers because they might ___15___ the inner tube.

Fix the valve in place with the valve nut.

Put the ___16___ back on the bike.

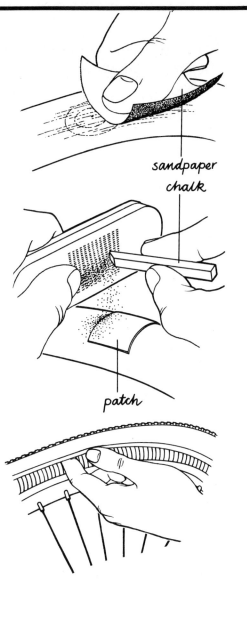

sandpaper

chalk

patch

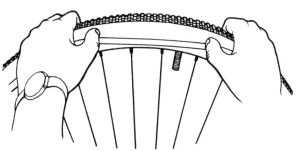

CLOZE

There was an accident at the road junction in the diagram.   The drivers involved made statements to the police.

What to do

Copy the diagram.   Read the statements on the next page.
Draw the cars in the right place on your diagram.   Use the key.

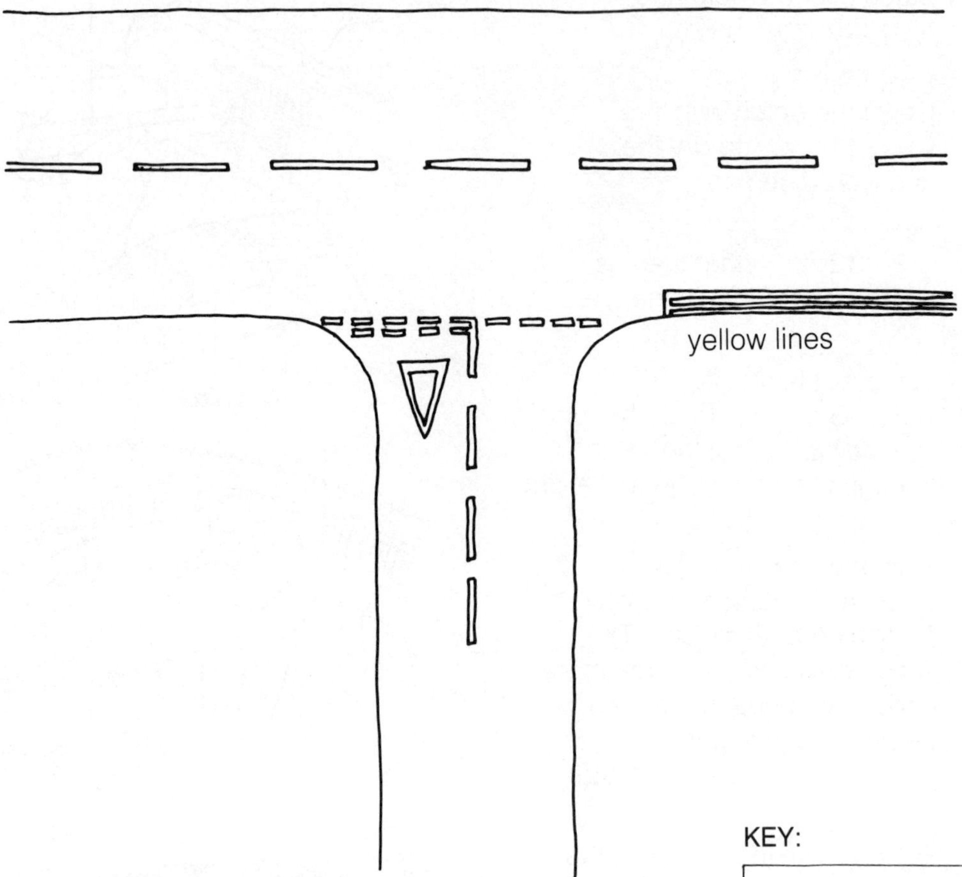

yellow lines

KEY:

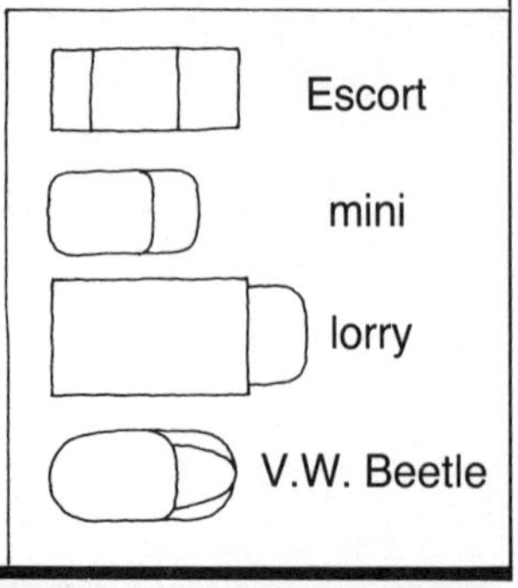

Escort	
mini	
lorry	
V.W. Beetle	

What to do next

Who do you think was to blame?

Statement 1 V.W. Beetle driver
I was helping my friend carry her shopping into her house. I know I was parked on double yellow lines, but I was only stopping for a minute. I was just getting back into the car when I heard a terrible noise. I looked up and saw the Escort swerve across the road and hit the lorry coming the other way. The driver of the Escort was lucky to be alive.

Statement 2 Mini driver
I was waiting to turn right. There was a car parked very close to the corner. I couldn't see if the road was clear so I pulled out slowly to the middle of the road. I couldn't see anything. Then suddenly the Escort came along. It swerved and hit the lorry that was coming the other way.

Statement 3 Escort driver
I was driving home from work. I had had a couple of drinks at the pub. I was passing a car parked near the corner. Suddenly I saw a yellow Mini in the middle of the road in front of me. I put on my brakes and swerved to miss it. I missed the Mini but I hit a lorry, coming the other way. I wasn't drunk. I don't know what the fool in the Mini was doing in the middle of the road.

Statement 4 Lorry driver
I was driving back to the depot. I was in a hurry to get home. All of a sudden I saw an Escort coming at me. I tried to stop but it was no use. He hit into the front of my lorry. His car was a write-off. It wasn't my fault, but the police will say it is. They always blame truck drivers.

This is a true story, or so they say.   It happened in a small village called Wardstone about six hundred years ago.   Wardstone was near a river.   There was a pool in the river called 'The Devil's Bowl'.   It was deep and dark and still.   Local people said it was bottomless and that it had swallowed up many people.   A strange mist always hung over the pool, even on warm sunny days.   No birds lived near the pool.   No animals came to drink there.   It had a sour and sinister atmosphere.

What to do

Find the missing words.   Write the number and the word you choose.

One fine September morning in 1360, a traveller came to Wardstone. His name was Joseph.   He was a wine-seller.   He went from house to house trying to   1   his fine red wine.   By the end of the day, he was   2   and needed somewhere to sleep.   He came to an old, empty   3   by the river.   It was dirty and rat-infested, but it was better than nothing.

The next   4   Joseph wanted to wash.   There was   5   water at the cottage so he went down to the river.   He came to that dark   6   known as 'The Devil's Bowl'.   The morning was very still and quiet.   A queer   .   7   hung over the pool.

Joseph took off his shirt and hung it over a thin, twisted tree that grew at the   ..   8   of the pool.   He bent down to wash his face.   He could see his   9   reflected in the dark, still water.

Then he got a terrible   10   .   As he   11   at his reflection, he saw it change!   His   12   went grey.   His eyes drooped.   His .   13   went wrinkled.   His teeth went   14   .   A   15   started to grow.

Joseph put his   16   to his face.   He thought he would   17   wrinkles and a beard.   But his own   .   18   felt quite normal.   Then he looked down at the   19   again.   It   20   an evil smile!   It wasn't his reflection.   There was a face under the water!

Joseph was very   .   21   .   He stood up.   He looked around for a rock.   He saw   22   at the water's edge.   He reached down for it but, as he did, a hand came up out of the water   23   grabbed his wrist.

Joseph was terrified.   The hand held his wrist like a steel
        24   .   He struggled in blind panic.   The pain was
unbearable.   The hand from under the water started to pull Joseph
down.   It   **25**   him nearer and nearer the water.   The hand
was trying to pull Joseph into the   **26**   !

Joseph reached out and grabbed the thin, twisted   **27**   by the
water's edge.   But his hand was   **28**   with terror and his
fingers lost their grip.   Now his face was   **29**   the water.

Joseph struggled with all his might   **30**   it was no use.   The
hand pulled him into 'The Devil's Bowl'.   The water closed over
him.   He struggled for his   **31**   .

Then a second evil claw grasped his neck.   The claws pulled him slowly
down to the   **32**   of the pool.   Water filled his lungs.   Looking
up, he saw a stream of   **33**   .   The last of his life was running
away.   Then there was nothing but darkness and the pool became a
mirror once more.

Later on that same day, a man from Wardstone was   **34**   'The
Devil's Bowl'.   He saw Joseph's   **35**   hanging on the thin,
twisted tree by the pool.   He left it there and went quickly on his way.

What to do

Read the story.   Some of the sentences are jumbled.   Find these sentences.   Put the words in the right order.   Write the sentences in your book.

Bill had just left school.   He was looking for a job.   He saw an advert in the local paper.   It said:

> ODD JOB MAN WANTED   RING 770829

Bill rang the number and fixed up an interview.   The man who put the advert in the paper was called Adams.   Him day Bill to the next see went.   Mr Adams liked the look of Bill so he offered him the job.   He said to Bill:

> "My work to want I in garden you.   I want you to work all this month – every day, Saturdays and Sundays.   I want you to work 31 days without a day off."

Bill agreed.   Was job a to get keen he.   He asked Mr Adams about the wages.

> "What do *you* think would be a fair wage?" said Adams.   Now when Bill had been at school, he had been top of the class at maths.   He idea had clever a.   Bill said:

> "You can pay me 1p. for the first day I work, 2p. for the second day I work, 4p. for the third day.   And so on.   Each day I work, I get double the pay from the day before.   You can pay me at the end of the month."

Mr Adams agreed.   He thought Bill was daft to work for such low wages.

The month at went Bill end of wages his for the.   He knocked on the door.   Mr Adams answered it.

> "I've come for my wages," said Bill.

> "How much do I owe you?" asked Adams, taking out his wallet.

> "£10,737,418 and 23p." said Bill with a smile.

Mr Adams fainted!   But Bill was right.   Wheelbarrow his home he wages in a took.

> **What to do**
>
> We asked some boys and girls this question:
> "If you could have one wish what would you wish for?"
> Here are their wishes.
> Classify them by copying the table and filling it in.

1.   Billy wished his mum and dad had a nice house.
2.   Sally wished she could swim very fast.
3.   Jimmy wished he could fly like Superman.
4.   Chris wished he had all the money in the world.
5.   Alison wished she had a hang glider and a pony.
6.   Tommy wished he had a room of his own at home.
7.   Shanta wished she had a real living dinosaur.
8.   Karen wished her name was Kate and not Karen.
9.   Brian wished he was good at maths.
10.   Julie wished that there were no more wars.
11.   Ali wished his granny was still alive.
12.   Linda wished she could be the first woman on the moon.
13.   Paula wished she had special powers like Wonder Woman.
14.   Bob wished he could find out who his real parents are.
15.   Jane wished that her mum and dad would stop arguing.

	1	2	3	4	5	6	7	8	9	10	11	12	13	14	15
Wishes that MIGHT come true															
Wishes that could NEVER come true															
Silly wishes															
Sensible wishes															

CLASSIFICATION

Some people from London use cockney rhyming slang when they talk together. Instead of the real word, they use some words that rhyme with it. For example, 'elephant's trunk' means drunk.

What to do

Match the cockney words on the left of the page with the meanings on the right. Write your answers like this:

1. Apples and pears = stairs

1.	Apples and pears	a)	hat
2.	Bacon and eggs	b)	house
3.	Bees and honey	c)	night
4.	Black and white	d)	knees
5.	Boat race	e)	face
6.	Bottle and stopper	f)	legs
7.	Bugs and fleas	g)	money
8.	Cat and mouse	h)	pound
9.	Lost and found	i)	kids
10.	Plates of meat	j)	feet
11.	Tit for tat	k)	stairs
12.	God forbids	l)	copper

Uncle Fred

Uncle Fred was always **elephant's trunk**.   He didn't have much **bees and honey**.   He was walking down James Street one day when he saw a man with an ugly **boat race**.   Uncle Fred put his **long and lingers** into the man's **bucket and float** pocket and stole his watch.   A **bottle and stopper** came up behind him and said,

"Evening all.   What's going on here?"

Uncle Fred turned round and stamped on the **bottle and stopper**'s **daisy roots**.   Uncle Fred ran down the **frog and toad** and got away on a **clever mike**.

The next **black and white**, Uncle Fred was **tiddly-winking** in the pub when he met the **bottle and stopper**.   The **bottle and stopper** said,

"Are you the man who stole the watch last **black and white**?"

Uncle Fred said,

"No it can't be me.   I wasn't in James Street."

The **bottle and stopper** said,

"You are a **holy friar**.   How do you know it happened in James Street?"

Uncle Fred was taken to the police station.

DEDUCTION

What to do

Some of the sentences in the story are jumbled.   Find these jumbled sentences.   Write them in your book so that they make sense.

Alison did a paper round.   She worked for Old Sam, the newsagent. She had to get up very early every day.   She had to be at the shop by 6 o'clock.   Sam's shop was at the top of a steep hill.   Of the was canal a bottom this at hill.

One dark November morning, when Alison got to the shop, she saw a red car parked outside.   The driver's door was open.
    "That's strange," Alison said to herself, "Sam has not got a car.
    The is wonder in I so shop who early?"

Alison looked in the shop door.   She got a shock.   Sam at masked a pointing man was a gun.   He was making the old man fill a bag with cigarettes.   Alison had to act fast.   She ran back to the red car.   Two got gutter of she matchsticks out the.   She pushed them into the car valves on the front wheels of the car.   The tyres hissed and started to go flat.

Then Alison ran down the hill to the phone box by the canal.   She called the police and told them about the robber in Sam's shop.   Came the hill just down car then the rushing red.   The front tyres were flat.   The masked man could not control the car.   It ran off the road.   Then it smashed into the phone box.   It rolled over into the canal.

The robber was unconscious.   Pulled the into Alison jumped to side him the and water.   Old Sam came running down the hill.   He helped Alison pull the robber out of the water.   He was hurt, but still alive.   The police arrived a few minutes later and took the man away.

What to do

Read the conversation.
What has been missed out?
Write out the missing parts.

Julie comes home from school.
Her dad is in the kitchen.

Julie	Hello Dad.
Dad	Hello Julie. You're home early. It is only 3 o'clock.
Julie	We got sent home.
Dad	_____ 1 _____
Julie	The heating went off. The school was like an ice box.
Dad	_____ 2 _____
Julie	Yes please. I need something to warm me up.
Dad	Come and sit by the fire.
Julie	Is Mum home yet?
Dad	No, she works late on Thursdays.
Julie	_____ 3 _____
Dad	At about six o'clock.
Julie	I wish I could stay at home all day like you, Dad.
Dad	_____ 4 _____
Julie	I hate school.
Dad	You would hate being unemployed. School isn't that bad. At least you see your mates every day.
Julie	Don't be sad, Dad. I hate it when you're miserable.
Dad	Then cheer me up.
Julie	How?
Dad	_____ 5 _____
Julie	I don't know any jokes.
Dad	Then I will tell you one: 'What's got six legs, two heads and goes to football matches?'
Julie	A football team?
Dad	_____ 6 _____
Julie	A space monster?
Dad	No.
Julie	_____ 7 _____
Dad	A mounted policeman.
Julie	Ugh! Your jokes are as bad as your cooking.
Dad	_____ 8 _____

CLOZE

What to do

We asked five people how they would rescue the rabbit from the well. This is what they said. Would their ideas work? If not why not?

Write your answers like this:

Alan's idea wouldn't work because . . . . .

Alan's idea

Get another pet rabbit. Put it in the bucket. The bucket will go to the bottom of the well. The first rabbit will jump into the bucket to be with its mate. Now pull up the bucket quickly.

William's idea

Put a carrot and a stone in the bucket at the top of the well. The bucket will go down to the bottom of the well. The rabbit will smell the carrot. It will jump into the bucket. Now quickly jump into the other bucket. This will go down very quickly. The rabbit will come to the top of the well.

Linda's idea

Find some thin string. Tie the carrot onto one end. Lower the carrot down the well. The rabbit will start eating the carrot. Pull the carrot slowly up. The rabbit will hold on tight with its teeth. Quickly pull the carrot and the rabbit to the top of the well.

Samantha's idea

Put some stones into the bucket. It will go down to the bottom of the well. Climb into the well. Grab the rope and climb down. Pick up the rabbit. Hold it tightly in your left hand. Climb back up the rope.

Sharon's idea

Put a stone into the bucket at the top of the well. The bucket will go down the well. Drop a lot of stones into the well. The water in the well will come up over the rock. The rabbit will jump into the bucket to keep dry. Now pull up the bucket.

Can you think of a better idea?

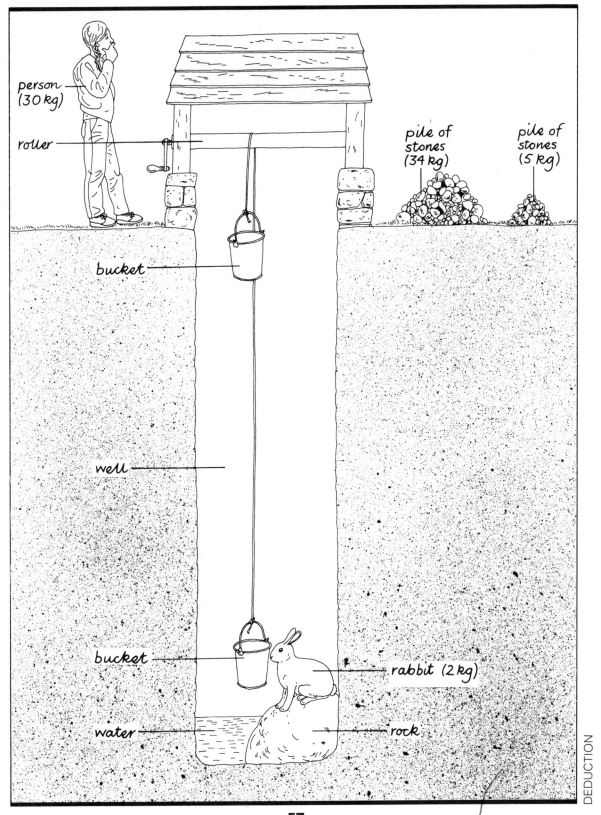

person
(30 kg)

roller

pile of
stones
(34 kg)

pile of
stones
(5 kg)

bucket

well

bucket

rabbit (2 kg)

water

rock

We asked eleven boys about their pocket money.
What they said is on the opposite page.
Are the sentences below true(T), false(F) or is there not enough
evidence(NEE)?

1. John Smith gets the same amount of pocket money every week.
2. Edward Burrow gets lots of comics.
3. Darren Walshaw saves most of his money.
4. Lee Carter has to work for his pocket money.
5. Andrew Martin likes swimming.
6. Lee Lamb has got a BMX bike.
7. Ravi Patel saves most of his pocket money.
8. Andrew Davison gets more pocket money than Andrew Perry.
9. Andrew Martin and Lee Lamb get the same amount of pocket money.
10. Sometimes Lee Carter gets as much money as Andrew Perry.
11. Simon Rowlins and Andrew Martin always buy sweets with their money.
12. John Smith always gets more money than Lee Lamb.
13. All the 14 year old boys get more than £2.
14. The two 12 year old boys have CB radios.
15. One of the 12 year old boys has got more than £20 saved.
16. None of the 14 year olds save any money.

DEDUCTION

Edward Burrow (11 yrs)
I don't get any pocket money.   My parents buy me sweets and things.

Lee Carter (12 yrs)
I earn my pocket money.   I help my mum.   If I work very hard I get
£1.   I save up for Christmas presents.

Andrew Davison (14 yrs)
I get £5 a week.   I buy books and football stuff.   I spend it all.

Lee Lamb (12 yrs)
I get £1 from my mum and £1 from my dad.   I usually buy a special
hamburger.   I also buy BMX magazines.

Andrew Martin (14 yrs)
I get £1 from my mum and dad.   I spend it on all sorts of things, like
sweets and comics.   Sometimes I go to the swimming baths.

Ravi Patel (11 yrs)
I get £3 – some from my grandad and some from my dad.   I save £2.   I
spend some money when I go out with my dad.

Andrew Perry (14 yrs)
I get £2 from my mum.   In summer I earn £25 a week.   I put some
money in the bank.   I hire 3 video cassettes for the weekend.   I play on
the slot machines or go for rides on trains.

Simon Rowlins (11 yrs)
I get 50p.   Sometimes I save up for parts for my bike.   Sometimes I buy
sweets.

John Smith (13 yrs)
Sometimes I get £3 and sometimes I get £2.   I get extra if I go shopping
for my mum.   I buy sweets, mod badges and worms for fishing.

Darren Walshaw (11 yrs)
I get £1.50.   I put £1 in the bank.   I spend 50p on toys.

Joseph Waters (9 yrs)
I get 50p.   I spend it on anything such as comics, sweets or sometimes
toys.

What to do

Angela had an interesting life.
The time line shows what happened in her lifetime.
Say if these statements are true(T), false(F), or if there is not
enough evidence(NEE).

1. Angela was born in a car.
2. Angela listened to the radio at school.
3. Angela got a T.V. when she retired.
4. Angela died before the first man went into space.
5. The first L.P. was made after Angela retired.
6. Angela was at college all through the First World War.
7. Angela retired during the Second World War.

Now answer these questions:

8. When were computers invented?
9. When did the first man go into space?
10. When was the first L.P. made?
11. How old was Angela when she left school?
12. How long was there between the two wars?
13. For how long was Angela unemployed?
14. How old was Angela when the first man went into space?

DEDUCTION

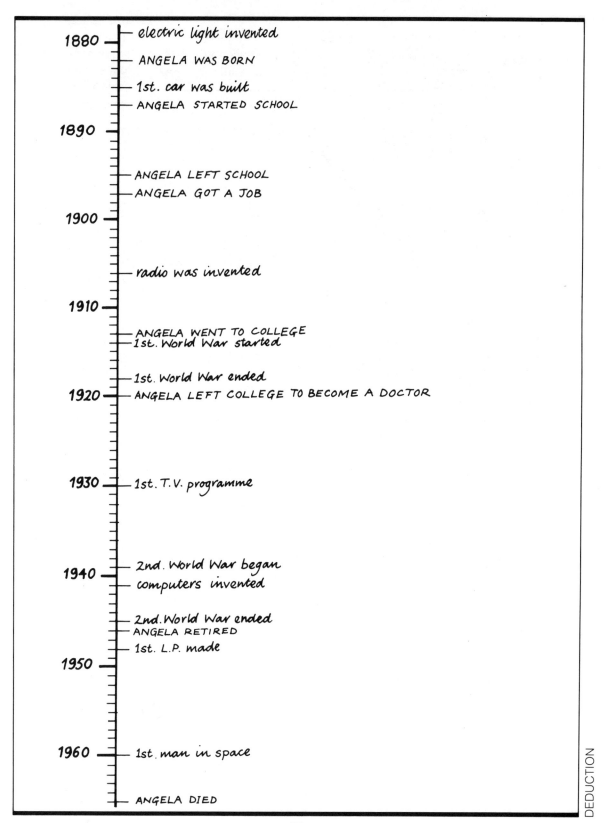

1880	electric light invented
	ANGELA WAS BORN
	1st. car was built
	ANGELA STARTED SCHOOL
1890	
	ANGELA LEFT SCHOOL
	ANGELA GOT A JOB
1900	
	radio was invented
1910	
	ANGELA WENT TO COLLEGE
	1st. World War started
	1st. World War ended
1920	ANGELA LEFT COLLEGE TO BECOME A DOCTOR
1930	1st. T.V. programme
1940	2nd. World War began
	computers invented
	2nd. World War ended
	ANGELA RETIRED
	1st. L.P. made
1950	
1960	1st. man in space
	ANGELA DIED

START → Light the oven at gas 4, 180°C. → Grease the cake tin. → Put 180 g margarine and 180 g sugar into a mixing bowl.

Sieve 180 g flour and 10 g cocoa onto a plate. ← Add the eggs and milk to the sugar and margarine. Mix together. ← Beat 3 eggs with 2 tablespoons of milk in a small bowl. ← Stir them together until the mixture is soft and creamy.

Add the flour and cocoa to the mixture of eggs, milk, margarine and sugar. Mix together. → Put the mixture into the cake tin. → Put the tin into the oven. → Wait for 40 minutes.

STOP ← When the knife comes out clean, put the cake onto a cooling tray. ← Stick a knife into the middle of the cake. ← Take the cake out of the oven.

What to do

This flow chart tells you how to make a cake. Use it to find the missing words. Write your answers like this: 1 Gas 4, 180°C

Method

Light the oven at   1   .   2   the cake tin. Put the   3   and sugar in a mixing bowl. Stir these together with a wooden spoon until the mixture is   4   and   5   . Beat the eggs and milk together with a fork. Add the eggs and   6   a bit at a time to the mixture. Stir the mixture for a short while. Sieve the flour and   7   together. Add the flour and   8   , a spoonful at a time, to the mixture. When the mixture is smooth, put it into the tin. Put it in the oven. Wait for   9   . Take out the cake. Test it with a   10   . If the   11   comes out   12   , the cake is ready. Tip the cake out onto a tray and leave to cool.

What to do next

Use the flow chart to make a list of ingredients.

What to do

Copy the map into your book.
Next to each home, write the name of the people who live there.
Say what kind of home it is.

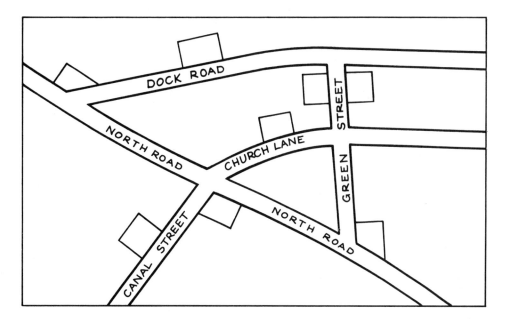

A.　Mr and Mrs Carter live on the corner of North Road and Dock Road.

B.　Mrs Clark lives on the corner of North Road and Green Street.

C.　If you turn into Green Street from Dock Road, you come to Mr Halliwell's house on your left.

D.　There is a caravan park in Dock Road.

E.　Mr Halliwell lives in a detached house.

F.　Mr and Mrs Patel live in the same street as Mr Halliwell.

G.　Mrs Clark lives in a terraced house.

H.　There is a very tall block of flats on the corner of Canal Street and North Road.

I.　Mr and Mrs Thompson live over a shop in Canal Street.

J.　Mr Leck lives in a bungalow in Church Lane.

K.　Mr Wilson lives in a caravan.

L.　The Patels and the Carters live in flats.

M.　Mr Kennon lives on the 22nd floor of a block of flats.

MATCHING

Amy had an accident when she was a child.   Her dad was parking the car.   He didn't see Amy playing in the road behind him.   He knocked her down.

Amy fell on her head.   She fractured her skull and damaged her brain.   One of the back wheels of the car went over her right hand.

Amy has never recovered.   She is paralysed down the left side of her body.   She cannot move her left arm or left leg.   Her right arm is not much use.   She cannot turn on taps or unscrew jars.   She can move her right arm from side to side.

Amy spends most of her time in a wheel chair.   She can't walk but she can stand up.   She can sit down by herself on a chair but not on the floor.   She cannot lie down or sit up without help.

What to do

Design a bath for Amy that she could use by herself.
To help you, copy the tables and fill them in.

part of body	how Amy can use that part of the body
right arm	
left arm	
right leg	
left leg	

activity	how your bath will help Amy
turn on the taps	
get into the bath	
get out of the bath	
lie down in the bath	
put on shampoo	
rinse her hair	

DRAWING